DEDICATED TO ALL EDUCATORS
THANK YOU FOR EDUCATING

25 Principles of Martial Arts

ISBN-13 9780983594604 (PRINT)
ISBN-13 9780983594611 (EBOOK)
Library of Congress Control Number:
2011928580(PRINT)
Copyright© 2011 by Mikazuki Publishing House
Author: Kambiz Mostofizadeh
Illustrations by: Hoornaz Mostofizadeh
Publisher: Mikazuki Publishing House

WARNING: DO NOT ATTEMPT ANY TECHNIQUES YOU SEE IN THIS BOOK UNLESS UNDER THE SUPERVISION OF A TRAINED MARTIAL ARTIST.

DISCLAIMER: THE PUBLISHER AND AUTHOR

ACCEPT NO RESPONSIBILITY FOR YOUR

ACTIONS BASED ON THIS BOOK.

The information contained within this book is for

educational and commercial purposes and does not

necessarily reflect the views of the publisher.

CONTENTS

INTRODUCTION

Having practiced martial arts for the majority of my life and having read many books related to martial arts, I was intrigued at the thought of a book that would synthesize the mode of thought in to a system that could be drawn upon by students. On my travels throughout Asia, I learned of and experienced many unique and delightful cultural customs and traditions. Martial arts is an ancient art form and cultural landmark of human triumph in the quest for self-preservation. The principles, philosophies, and study of martial arts have existed for thousands of years and have been discussed by Sun Tzu, Lao Tzu, Miyamoto Musashi, Von Clausewitz, Machiavelli, and others. The great breadth of knowledge contained among so many great writers and leaders humbled me with the idea of creating one book that would be able to entirely explain the principles of martial arts. I understood the ambitious task before me and entered in to it with great humility. I invite you to read and enjoy the 25 Principles of Martial Arts and hope that you will find the same satisfaction in reading it as I did in writing it.

1st Principle of Formlessness

The Principle of Formlessness depends on concealing your actions, moves, techniques, operations, abilities, thoughts, processes, and actions until the very last moment.   In individual combat, your opponent will attempt to read your defenses and will try to foil your actions if you give off signals notifying your opponent of your attack. When the opponent is able to see your form, they are able to perceive your gaps. This will give your opponent the advantage when attacking you. If the opponent is unable to see your form, they are unable to find your gaps, making your vulnerabilities hidden. If your vulnerabilities are exposed, then your weaknesses are exposed. Not revealing your shape or form, forces the opponent to have to guess what you are doing, which frustrates them, and forces them to make mistakes they would not normally make. In contrast, if you are able to see the form of your opponent, then attacking them is easier because their vulnerabilities become apparent to you, thus allowing you to develop strategies that are based on your opponent, rather than pre-decided strategies. Taking a strategy that has been successful previously, and applying it to another situation, with the belief that it will work again, is pure folly. It will most likely result in your loss, because the strategy was not tailored to you and your opponent's situation.

The advantage of surprise is easily gained through the application of the Principle of Formlessness. Large amount of resources and more individuals in your organization do not necessarily equate to victory over your opponent if you have lost the advantage of formlessness. This is because your opponent will prepare and ready themselves with defenses which may counterbalance your attack, essentially nullifying your actions. The silence of your actions hide your form and confuse your opponents. If you want to have the advantage of surprise and deny your enemies or opponents the opportunity to prevent your progression, be very careful to mask your actions and reveal no form. In group combat operations, the force that reveals their position, reveals their power, reveals their forces, makes themselves vulnerable and open to their opponent's advances. Hiding your form has the advantage also of denying your opponents the opportunity to make an assessment of your strength, thereby denying them knowledge. If your form is revealed, it does not always lead to your defeat, but it may reveal the intricacies of your inner workings, thereby negating your strategy. You can, however, use smaller actions to distract your opponent in order

to mask your larger action.

2nd Principle of Yielding

The 2nd Principle of Yielding teaches us not to

force an issue, to not attempt to meet force with force, and to not use force in the place of finesse. The technical application of a Juji-Gatame or an Armbar in individual combat, applies the whole of the body weight of an individual, against the weight of the opponent's arm. The 2nd Principle of Yielding states that the opponent's force should not be met head on with force, but to use the blending of forces so you can control the opponent. In relationships, often it is the yielding of one partner, that creates counterforce for receiving the advantage. The individual that yields on the mat or in real life gains the advantage because, the inevitable opportunity will arise that will allow the individual that has previously yielded to derive greater power.

Yielding is the opposite of "standing your

ground", although yielding is not permanently

retreating. Yielding is not permanent, but rather a

temporary action that uses strategy to seemingly put

the opponent in the advantage for a short period of

time. Martial arts principles subscribe to the duality of forces as witnessed in strikes and defenses, throws and counter-throws, and holds and escapes. The opponent's advantage quickly disappears because your yielding creates the opportunity for you to focus the bulk of your strength against the weakest parts of your opponent. (For ex. joints & throat) Yielding is being pliable and flexible. Each situation demands its own answer and approach. In many situations, it is normal to be rigid however, by yielding you are gaining the advantage.

When you are yielding, your opponent gains a false sense of confidence which ruins their defensive thought processes. This results in the opponent attacking without gauging the consequences of their actions. In individual combat, the action of pivoting and stepping out of the way of an attack is yielding. When an opponent pushes you and you pull the opponent while turning, this is yielding. When an opponent pulls you and you push while turning, this is yielding. The average opponent, not trained in martial arts that use yielding including Aikido, Jujitsu, Judo and others, will attempt to use strength to strike you , throw you, lock your joints, or choke you.

The reliance of pure yielding will defeat the mixed use of strength and yielding. Yielding in its essence, makes the applier of its principle an elusive opponent because, your opponent's cannot strike or control what has no base to be attacked. If I move forward and you move in to me, it is easier to yield. You cannot yield against that which you cannot touch. In group combat, yielding would be similar to the 10th Principle of Retreating, with the key difference being that the 2nd Principle of Yielding does not create permanent retreat, but temporarily creates time and space for using leverage to concentrate your force

using flanking (angled, unorthodox, unpredictable)

movements. The goal is to reverse the weakness that

you possess and be able to convert this into a

strength that will work in your favor.

3rd Principle of Fast Loss, Quick Win

The 3rd Principle of Fast Loss, Quick Win
teaches that a fast loss or a fast win is more
advantageous to you than a slow win and slow loss.
A fast loss is commendable and allows you to be able
to reflect while asking questions that will allow you to
reach a greater understanding. A fast win allows you
to conserve resources to be stronger for the next
phase, and reduces your vulnerability. A slow win
drains your resources, tires your forces(arms, legs),
and makes you vulnerable to a greater amount of
injury. A slow loss also has similar consequences as
the slow win, but has the added attribute of loss.
Despite being able to reflect afterward on the reasons
for the slow loss, you did ultimately lose.

A long dragged out victory makes you weak

despite it having the result of also making your opponent weak. Similar to attrition, you would still be at a disadvantage if your opponent has more resources than you do. It is therefore in your best interest to not attempt to compete unless you are ready, prepared, and capable to execute a quick win or fast loss. Determination does create certain amount of momentum that can propel you forward but, resources are the key to maintaining the campaign. It is also an unfortunate reality, that it may be difficult to exactly gauge the amounts of resources needed to complete the task, so you should attempt to plan for this. You will lose or waste resources by attempting to win in an unwinnable situation. A fast loss allows you to progress because you no longer have to expend resources. Conserve your resources for a later time when you may have the possibility of

achieving a quick win. The slow loss will only put you at a disadvantage in the long run because when the actual opportunity arrives in which you could exploit, you would have less resources to achieve a "critical mass" to substantially affect the situation. In many situations, to walk away or retreat is honorable and not shameful, but quite admirable.

4th Principle of Deflection

The 4th Principle of Deflection has some similarities to the 2nd Principle of Yielding. In individual combat, the use of deflection is executed using blocking techniques ranging from outer blocks, upper blocks, lower blocks, parry blocks, etc. These blocks similar to the 2nd Principle, do meet force using with force, but also attempt to blend with the incoming force, ultimately causing the force to change its trajectory. The reverse punch strike being thrown at your chin by the opponent can only change trajectory if the force is deflected. The deflection causes the trajectory of the incoming strike to move making it miss your chin. If the strike was not deflected, it would hit your chin. In group combat, deflection uses the tactics of diversion in order to trick your opponent as to your real intentions. The 1st Principle of

Formlessness shares similarities with the 4th Principle

of Deflection with the key difference being that in the

4th Principle, you are not hiding your form but showing

a false form. In the 4th Principle, your form is not

hidden from the opponent, but used to re-direct the

opponent's energy away from you so that the

opponent cannot affect you. Your opponent may be

stronger than you giving you a disadvantage, but by

using the 4th Principle of Deflection, you are redirecting the incoming force of the opponent forcefully. It is easier to move the opponent from their weakest point and deflection has such a goal. In the application of this principle, you should attempt to use the force of the opponent to yield temporarily, while channeling their force in the direction you desire.

5th Principle of Division

In the 5th Principle of Division, your opponent 's strength can be divided, while your strength is whole.

Your opponent is divided because they have to attempt to defend everywhere simultaneously because they are unable to foresee where the next move will be. The way you divide your enemy, is by causing doubt in their hearts to win. By executing fast and rapid advancement, your opponents will be frozen, despite having seen your form. The reason they are frozen and hesitant is because your unpredictability divides their forces, as they brace for your advancement. The way to divide your enemy is to cause them to doubt their own abilities to be able to effectively attack you. If they divide their forces in half, they are at half strength. If they divide their forces in to 10 groups, then each one of those 10 groups is only 1/10 of the total force. This gives you the advantage because you are able to concentrate larger amounts of force against smaller amounts in turn, ensuring yourself of a much easier victory.

6th Principle of Circling

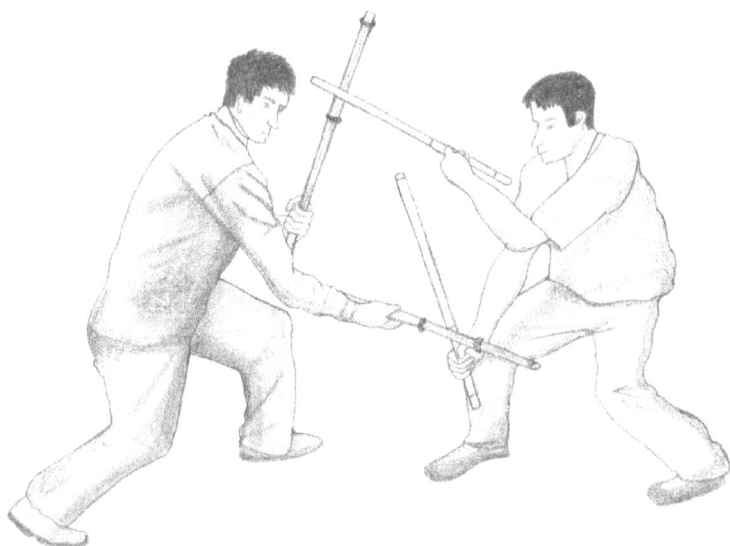

The 6th Principle of Circling teaches us that

spinning or moving around our axis while the

opponent is close causes the opponent to become

entangled. It also causes the opponent to lose their

balance. The 6th Principle also includes evasion of

strikes. To circle is to evade and to cause your

opponent difficulties in attempting techniques against

you. The 6th Principle of Circling is to move toward the weak side of the opponent. The 6th principle of Circling has similarities with the 2nd Principle of Yielding with the difference being that the 6th Principle is intended for evading to counter, while the 2nd Principle's is a purposeful movement with the intended purpose of retreating temporarily.

By circling, you create a much harder target for your opponent to attack, because your centerline is constantly shifting. The circular motions are meant to disrupt your opponent's attempt to target where they will strike. It also confuses your opponent and causes them to have waste precious time thinking of the area to target. This is the reason that the 6th Principle of Circling, is a defensive principle rather than an offensive principle. Whether you are evading a

punch, evading a kick, evading a weapon attack, evading a takedown attempt, or escaping from the hold of an opponent, you are utilizing the 6th Principle of Circling. In individual combat, the 6th Principle of Circling is to move with the belief that the opponent wants your centerline at a position where attacking you is most optimal. However, by your movements of circling on the weaker side of the opponent, you not only confuse your opponent by showing a false form, but also avoid the brunt of any heavy blows your opponent attempts, since they will no longer be in a position to effectively cause you any harm. The speed generated by the body's rotation will generate strength. This force generated from the rotation will disrupt the concentration of the opponent, hurl the opponent if they are too close, and most importantly keep your maneuvers evasive so as to frustrate the opponent.

7th Principle of Straight Lines

The 7th Principle of Straight Lines teaches that the closest trajectory between two points is a straight one. In individual combat, you may be attacked by a hook punch but counter successfully with a jab, despite the fact that your strike started after your opponent's. On the other hand, you may attempt to strike your opponent with a mid-level roundhouse kick, but your opponent may still be able to front kick you successfully and effectively despite the fact that they started striking after you.

The 7th Principle of Straight Lines dictates that the dominance of straight line attacks give some styles such as Wing Chun an advantage in striking from punching range. Wing Chun specializes in centerline attacks and its practitioners focus their vision on the opponent's center. When entering towards an opponent with the purpose of grabbing them in order to clinch or hold their body, straight line angles are utilized by grapplers. Boxers rely on straight line attacks as the jab remains the dominant

punch attempted and landed in most pugilistic

contests. Fencing also relies on straight line attacks

and circular movements are prohibited. Lunging

attacks such as lunging punching strikes or lunging

knee strikes use projection and movement in straight

lines. In many throws in Judo, when entering to off

balance or throw, practitioners move in straight lines.

8th Principle of Balance

The 8th Principle of Balance teaches us that for every action that we do, there must be an opposite reaction. Using the principles of a wheelbarrow, you will pull up on one lever and oppositely push down on the other lever in order to turn or flip. The 8th Principle of Balance also can be applied to your being as well. When you train your body for two hours a day, you should also stimulate your mind for the same amount of time. If you punch in a fight, you should also kick. If you push, you should push in order to adhere to the way of balance. Balance is important in multiple settings, from diet and nutrition, combat, academics, and entertainment. The importance of balance is to ensure that a well rounded approach is taken to individual growth. Balancing the activities of the mind with the activities of the body will allow you to receive a balanced approach in your life. Overconsumption and aiming for excess is unhealthy and creates problems by focusing on desires. A balanced life allows the individual to achieve peace of mind. Solely focusing on the attainment of material items deprives you of your spirituality. An excess in one area, leaves you with deficiency in another. One simply cannot only have an emphasis on one single area or else the whole balance is off. You wouldn't be able to win a marathon if you sprinted all the way through and conversely you wouldn't win the race if you simply walked toward the finish line. Balance also teaches us by way of experience, that through its practice, you can accomplish many great things. For example, boxers train both their arms as well as their core in order to both attack and also be able to absorb heavy blows.

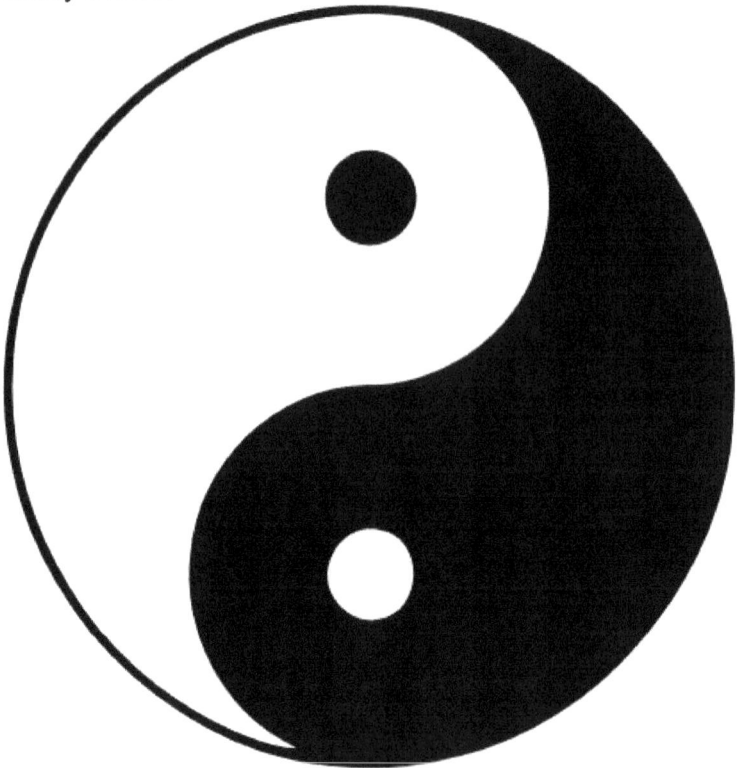

Their training revolves around a balance of taking blows as well as receiving blows. Many people complain about being on a losing streak or that they are experiencing bad luck because of such a loss. What has to be understood is that loss is followed by gain. There are cycles in gain and loss ultimately balancing each other out. The 8th Principle of

Balance is an essential Principle for every martial arts practitioner because it relays to you the essential element for living a fruitful life.

9th Principle of Avoiding Conflict

The 9th Principle of Avoiding Conflict teaches us that it is always advantageous to win without fighting. This can be done in a multiple of ways. One way is by not engaging at all, whether it is verbal or in actual combat. Fighting consumes resources including time, money and even energy. If you can avoid conflict, then doing so will later give you an advantage. This will anger and frustrate the mind of the opponent, but will not hurt your forces. Not engaging means to not respond to verbal and if possible, attempted physical attacks. It is easy to become entangled, but it takes willpower and mental strength to disengage. Emotionally controlling oneself by maintaining inner peace is essential to avoiding conflict. Conflicts are easily started and are quickly escalated or progressed through a series of incidents. Each incident helps to escalate the overall conflict resulting in greater tension. It is obviously more difficult to de-fuse a situation however, the right words and phrases could help to bring both sides closer to an understanding. Setting limits is a logical way for presenting your position, but being inflexible makes the application of this principle difficult to implement. Flexibility is an essential pre-requisite to avoiding conflict.

The de-escalation and gradual disengagement between two opposing forces may not result in peace,

but the effort put forth to de-escalate does assist in

the creation of an atmosphere that that is conducive

to peace. The initiator of a conflict is acting in one

form or another as an aggressor and therefore the

defender will seek to avoid conflict despite simultaneously seeking to defend. The act of disengagement and avoiding conflict, is not the act of retreating. Avoiding conflict is thinking and planning many steps ahead so as to not be in a position at any point that would jeopardize your strength and position, making you vulnerable. The key in avoiding conflict is being able to recognize the planted seeds of conflict before they grow, thereby preventing future conflict from arising. In order to acquire mastery in being able to pinpoint or identify the beginning stages of conflict, you have to recognize the symptoms that are visibly noticeable to your observations.

10th Principle of Retreating

The 10th Principle of Retreating teaches us that you may not always be prepared for a situation, therefore be ready at any time to move back to planning.

You retreat despite having the courage, willpower, and determination to move forward because your lacking in elements that will contribute to your success. Winning is a matter of having the correct combinations of factors working in your favor and choosing to retreat does not equal loss. It is sometimes more advantageous to retreat because by retreating you are conserving the remaining resources you have until you are able to effectively advance. Although we wish to advance always, the option of retreating should never be abandoned and the use of the 10th Principle of Retreating will strengthen its practicioner. For the most part, retreating has been associated as a sign of weakness, but if analyzed properly, it will become an important option that any leader should use to exit an un-advantageous situation.

Conflicts like competitive races are zero sum games, meaning that there is one winner and one loser. This also means that the winner will win at the expense of the loser. If there is no engagement because one party to the conflict has retreated, the remaining party will only consume resources and create opportunities for inner discord among its own members by not also retreating. This is precisely the reason why smaller companies are able to compete with larger companies and why guerrillas are able to effectively combat regular armies. The retreat by one party, will in most cases, leave the other party more vulnerable, not less. This is because the remaining party has to retreat or remain stagnant thereby consuming vital resources, squandering funds, and creating opportunities for internal rivalries to grow from stagnation.

11th Principle of Minimal Exertion

The 11th Principle of Minimal Exertion teaches us that more strength does not equate to more effectiveness and that using less strength will create greater effectiveness. This principle emphasizes technique and intelligence rather than strength. A Judo practicioner best applies this principle through throwing techniques in which one person hurls a larger individual. Jujitsu practitioners apply bone breaking arm locks and even karate practitioners use simple wrist locks in self defense. Hapkido, Aikido, and many other grappling styles adhere to this effective principle. Martial arts teaches inner strength and resilience, allowing a smaller practicioner to use technique to triumph over brute force.

Jigoro Kano, the founder of Judo and a former

practicioner of Kito Ryu Jujitsu, specialized in throwing techniques which he introduced through this principle to the mainstream. Fluidity in martial arts is a key to being able to adapt to unforeseen and likely uncontrollable situations. This fluidity and adaptability is essential to maintaining a stable and clear mind during difficult situations. The 11th Principle of Minimal Exertion is about using proper application and technique in order to affect or control the situation. Momentum is a force that should blended with to benefit, but to move against the force of momentum would not only be nearly impossible, you would likely expend large amounts of resources doing so. Excessive movements and unrelated motions sap the strength of practitioners causing them to waste vital resources. By blending with the force, you can control the force with minimal exertion. The difficulty lies in finding the proper balance between technique and the least amount of strength exerted. Rely on technique and preparation and you will be ready for the challenge, but be careful not to allow yourself to become too cautious in waiting for the right opportunity or else you might become hesitant to take any action.

12th Principle of Self Cultivation

The 12th Principle of Non-Interference teaches us that martial skills require as much training time outside the training hall as they do inside. Martial skills are developed from time spent on the training mat or Tatami as they're taught by the Instructor. It is the dedication to self progress outside the training hall that creates the real progress as long as the principles acquired within the training hall are faithfully

applied outside the training hall.   Morehei Ueshiba,

the founder of Aikido, was a student of Sokaku

Takeda, but most martial arts scholars can agree that

Ueshiba was self-taught. The greatest swordsman in

the history of Japan, Miyamoto Musashi, was also self

taught. Determination to progress, can't be taught in

a school, but skills are. Determination to grow comes

from within propelling the student to seek knowledge

by following his/her passion.   Martial skills are

acquired in training halls and implemented rarely except in times of self defense. Although the training hall has many advantages including the ability to train with multiple partners, it is in many ways unrealistic to real life and death situations that have no rules. It is unrealistic that you will be driving your car barefoot or that you will be walking on the street barefoot. It is essential for a martial art student to dedicate time to pursuing progress in the martial art they're practicing. Self training depends on non-interference of any constraining factors and motivation, yet it is the initial interference or guidance by the teach that pushes the subject in to action.

The 14th Principle refers to the cultivation of the ideal qualities of the internal character including the development of the ideals of compassion, respect, charity, and honor. It teaches that cultivating the body should be done with the intention of cultivating the mind. The cultivation of a balanced nature that is hard or tough on the outside and soft or flexible on the inside, is the goal of this principle.

13th Principle of Defeat

The 13th Principle of Defeat teaches us that a loss is not a setback, but rather a step forward. Although you experienced a loss, have you really lost anything? You may have invested your time and money to gain first- hand experience in a matter, but did you really lose? Nay, it must be argued that you have gained. You have gained experience, that time and money were invested for you to gain. As bitter as a defeat is, it is really an opportunity for reflection in order for you to continue progression. In Judo, it is taught that in order for you to learn how to throw, you must first learn how to fall. Defeat is not failure because failure is a permanent state in contrast to defeat which is a transitory and temporary state. You are not a failure because you experienced defeat. It

is rather the opposite in that, you are a winner because you experienced defeat and now you know what not to do. Experience is gained at cost and this is why lessons should be drawn from the defeat, rather than seeking individuals to blame. Defeat is a teacher that strengthens our resolves and provides us with the necessary lessons for victory. To focus on your defeat with the aim of blaming, is a waste of energy. Drawing lessons from defeat is vital. The aim of the 13th Principle is to savor defeat as much or more than victory, in order for you to draw lessons from the experience and thus not repeat it. Why do we forget about our victories and focus on the defeats? If an individual has never lost, they will be crushed after they lose for the first time, because they will take longer to recover. Individuals that have experienced defeat, are better able to cope with the stress and in turn will be able to recover faster. Defeats are bitter situations, but despite the negative reputation attached to being defeated, greater importance should be given to the process undertaken and not the end result.

14th Principle of Timing

The 14th Principle of Timing teaches us in order for a defensive or offensive maneuver to be successful, the proper timing must be implemented. In boxing strategy, counterpunching and exploiting gaps depend on the 14th Principle of Timing. Although an opponent seem within range of your attack, your timing dictates the success of the strike. This is because your opponent is most likely not going to stand still while you strike them, so you may be facing a moving target. To strike your opponent where he/she is now would not be satisfactory because there is great potential that your opponent will be moving. This forces you to strike them where they are going to be, not where they currently are. To understand timing takes focused practice and

attention to detail. Karate practitioners utilize outside hook blocks to stop punches or kicks. Karate practitioners or Karateka practice for hundreds of hours to be able to block with proper timing. Taekwondo practitioners spend hundreds of hours practicing jumping flying kicks that depend on timing to hit their target. A strike thrown too early could cause you to miss thus off balancing you. A strike thrown too early could also cause you to waste resources for minimal gain thus making your action useless. A strike thrown too late could have greater consequences for you, including making you vulnerable to being hit by your opponent.   Timing is an essential element of martial arts and will continue to influence the way that martial arts are learned. Timing depends on the individual's awareness of space, so that their previous training will prepare them for initiating eye-hand coordination. By practicing daily and analyzing the nuances of timing , you will better understand the applications of the 14th Principle of Timing.

15th Principle of Movement

The 15th Principle of Movement teaches us that in order for victory, you must stay active. For you to secure victory, you must be more active than your opponent. You must be active, while they are resting. You must stay in motion and constantly maneuver around your opponent freely. This gives you the advantage and the momentum to reach success. It is an understandable fact that the size of your opponent will dictate the speed of their movement. It is this gap in their speed of movement that you will exploit to your advantage. Your movements need not be exceedingly fast to maneuver against your opponent. Your movements should be in a manner that causes your opponent to be surprised. There are two main types of movements, the orthodox and the unorthodox. Orthodox movements depend on predictable behavior like the movement of Karateka or a Boxer. Orthodox movements are well known and will not cause a surprise or create a stir in the stance of your opponent. Orthodox movements include frontal strikes in contrast to unorthodox movements that depend on flanking attacks or attacks from the sides.

Unorthodox movements are unpredictable and difficult for the opponent to defend against, like the strikes of a Drunken Kung Fu Master. Unorthodox movements confuse your opponents and cause them to have focus on defense because they cannot predict where your movement will be next. This frustrates and foils the attack of the opponent causing them to retreat, even if temporarily. Unorthodox movements can be used alone or to increase their effectiveness, can be used with orthodox movements. The Shaolin Monks travelled frequently, with sometimes only a 5 foot

wooden staff, but were known to use unorthodox

strikes to disrupt the attention & concentration of their

opponents. It is the mixture of orthodox and

unorthodox movements which give you the advantage

over your opponent. It is virtually impossible for your

opponent to plan to defend , if they are unsure of

where the next place you will attack. This is why the

mastery of the 15th Principle of Movement is so vital.

16th Principle of Mind States

The 16th Principle of Mind States teaches us that you can control and by will change your mind states in order to achieve success. Sobriety is a mind state as is drunkenness. You are what you fill your mind with. You are able to change from angry to happy in one instant. You can also change your mind state from happy to depressed in one instant. You have the ability to effect how you view the world by altering your perception in relation to the world. But first, it is important to understand what your mind states are. Your mind states are temporary and thus changeable by you when you decide you want it to change. Sometimes, individuals draw upon memories to change mind states and memories can also be triggered by a sensory input (smell, sound, etc).

Possessing the ability to be able to reset your mind

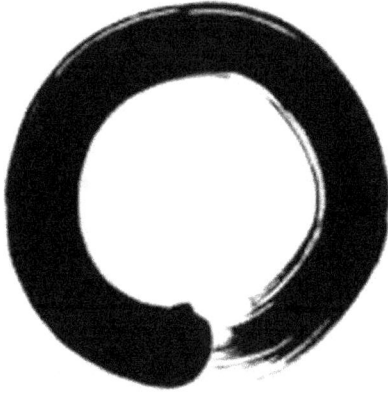

state at will when you are frustrated or stuck in a

position where you are not advancing, is most

advantageous. Meditation and purposeful breathing

exercises help to "clear the mind" of temporary states

in order to reach for a balanced mind state. In

meditation, it is the focus that assists the individual

that is meditating in achieving a balanced mind state.

Mind states are temporary and changeable by you,

because they are based on your emotions. Have you

ever witnessed an individual crying and laughing

within a very short period of time? The 16th Principle

of Mind States teaches that you can control your mind states by making the active decision to control your emotional states and calming your mind.

17th Principle of Memory

The 17th Principle of Memory teaches us that martial arts depend on memory for their successful implementation. The 17th Principle is achieved through the practice of Kata or a set of pre-defined movements and sparring for the purpose of training muscle and mind memory. The coordination of the muscles and mind working in tandem repetitiously, help to permanently train the practicioner in the knowledge and application of the movements . Kata is taught in steps and each new step is a building block on the foundation of the previous step. This is how difficult and complex sets of movements are taught and learned in the martial arts. Many martial arts scholars have stated the maxim "You will fight how you train" is true. Your body and mind in coordination adjust to the training conditions used. Sparring with different opponents allows individuals to not only adapt to fighting different body sizes, but more importantly trains the mind and muscle memory of the practicioner to various body heights. Kata teaches through pre-defined movements the applications and gives experience to the practicioner, making the movements almost second nature. The 17th Principle of Memory compliments and assists the 15th Principle of Movement.

18th Principle of Concentrated Attacks

The 18th Principle of Concentrated Attacks

teaches us that to divide resources makes the attack significantly weaker and may result in weakening the attacker permanently. By dividing your forces, you are dividing your resources, thus cutting your strength before you have even started. A concentrated attack has the advantage of utilizing all resources at its disposal, while a divided force is at half strength with twice the vulnerability. The more resources dedicated to one attack, the greater the momentum you will have and the stronger your force will be.

Since your resources are finite and limited you will have to maintain your strength. It is easy to divide resources and fail to create a reserve. In such times, it is better to re-group and consolidate resources. In striking arts including boxing, boxers train for hundreds of hours, focusing on striking the chin. Many boxing matches have ended with one well placed uppercut to the chin. Jujitsu applies the 18th

Principle of Martial Arts by focusing the whole weight of your body against an arm of your opponent. You attack is concentrated in that your entire body is essentially fighting against just his/her arm. In Wing Chun, punching is focused on the nose, chin, or throat of the opponent. In Kenpo Karate, kicking strikes are aimed at vital points including the knees and groin. When you divide your forces and divide your strength you weaken your position and create gaps for your opponent to exploit. When your opponent divides their forces, they create open gaps for you to exploit. The 18th Principle of Concentrated Attacks teaches you to consolidate and strengthen your position by maintaining focus and unity of purpose.

19th Principle of Total Defensibility

The 19th Principle of Total Defensibility teaches

us to defend areas that provide open gaps for the opponent to exploit. It is impossible to be able to defend all areas, but vital areas should be defended so as to not present openings for your opponent(s) to exploit. Although it is difficult to predict where you will be attacked, you can build initial defenses in order to protect areas of greater importance thereby negating your opponent's attack. Because there are only two ways your opponent could maneuver against you, predictably and unpredictably, it is the preparation you have invested beforehand which protects your position. Opponents make use of your gaps, but can

achieve no progress when there is nothing to be

exploited. The way to achieve total defensibility is to

prepare extensively beforehand so that there are no

surprises. The opposite implementation of this

principle is to exploit the gaps of your opponent

thereby causing them surprise. When are you are

attacked, your gaps are providing the opening for

exploitation so that your opponent gains from what

you were unable to defend. Because you have pre-

conceived beliefs based on your analysis or studies

where the attack will come from, you adapt your

defenses accordingly. If the opponent implements an

unpredictable action, it is difficult for you to defend

where you were unprepared to defend. The same rings true for your opponent as well. Unorthodox attacks are difficult to defend against *because* they are unpredictable. The predictability of your opponent gives you the cue on which defensive posture to take.

20th Principle of Alliances

The 20th Principle of Alliances teaches us that alliances are constantly shifting and changing because they are based on human desires. An alliance between yourself and a supporter was developed over time therefore resources were invested to develop it. The alliance is as fragile as it is temporary. The alliance you developed with your supporter was built on feelings and considerations of

mutual dependence. The alliance was also built on trust and a sense of mutual gain. As long as both sides see the opportunity for mutual gain and share a mutual understanding, there will be progress. The need for human beings to establish domain over their belongings is natural and should not be discounted. It is when the mutual understanding breaks down that the alliance begins to dissipate. The alliance is just a vehicle for mutual benefit and as the realization develops that less benefit is gained from the alliance, the alliance ceases to hold the same level of importance, that it had during its start. Your supporter or ally will have their own desires and wants regarding their level of involvement, adherence to the rules of the alliance, the hierarchal structure of the alliance, and the way in which the gains are distributed amongst each ally. It is for this reason that alliances are made with individuals that are of greater strength, rather than weaker. By making an effective alliance with an individual of greater strength, you are stronger because of this alliance. You are stronger because you now have access to resources that were previously unavailable to you. By making alliances with individuals that are weaker than yourself, you can benefit, although it may result in you being weakened by the exchange. However the arrangement, without trust, it is difficult for any alliance to make any progress. True alliances rely on real trust and conviction in the decision to align for the creation of greater power. But in order for the opposing party in the negotiation or alliance to be able to begin to trust you, first you must be willing to give your trust by trusting in them. The matter of effectively negotiating an alliance will determine the future outcome of the alliance. It will also allow an amicable withdrawal from the alliance if mutual understanding begins to dissipate. One sided negotiations fail to create alliances and even if one side agrees, the residue remaining from such negotiations, may leave behind feelings of mistrust. There may be certain times that you will need your partner in the alliance to give their

support. It is at these times that the unity and "worth"

of the alliance are tested. If your ally fails to help you

during times of crisis or when you are truly in need,

how can you depend on this ally's help in the future?

21st Principle of Shifting Power

The 21st Principle of Shifting Power teaches us that no one can indefinitely hold power because power is transitory. If you try to control power, you will become controlled by power. Power is elusive and shifting constantly. Powers stems from resources, since resources are limited and competition is vast, but power shifts because resources shift. Resources are moved, exchanged, and used to deny or give power to individuals or groups. Resources shift through exchange and with this exchange, power is also exchanged. Power is enhanced through the distribution of resources and power is deprived by denying resources. The

creation of power is through the creation of resources.

Alliances assist in the creation of power but also may

sap the strength of one ally causing the exchange of

power. Power is a zero sum game, in that, power

shifts through exchange from one body to another but

rarely is power created except by the creation of new

resources. Power is mostly shifted not created.

Your ability to potentially gather supporters is a sign

of power. Power can be drawn from having

supporters, but since that power is constantly shifting,

your supporters may be constantly changing.

Supporters are helpful in assisting to legitimize your power but, they can create more problems than benefits, if not handled properly. You should use the 21st Principle of Shifting Power to create the opportunity for you to be on the receiving end in the exchange of power.

22nd Principle of Hard & Soft

The 22nd Principle of Hard & Soft teaches us that opposite forces balance each other out. Hard strikes cannot be met with hard defenses because the harder strike will win. Hard strikes, for example, a roundhouse kick to the thigh of the opponent, would not be met with a hard defense. The roundhouse kick would be "checked" by the opponent raising their leg and knee to deflect the kick. This is a prime example of hard being balanced with soft. A striker whose sole purpose is strikes that are hard, can be defeated by a pure grappler whose style is soft. By hard, I mean using strikes and by soft, I mean being pliable/flexible or yielding as in the techniques used in jujitsu. In negotiations you can also be hard or soft. When you are hard, you are asking for concessions and when you are soft you are yielding. But by being soft or pliable/flexible, you are creating an opportunity in the future for you to cause the opponent to bend to your will. Being forceful is being hard because you are not yielding, but rather causing others to yield for you. Being hard is using aggression to meet aggression. Being soft is using yielding, deflection, circling, and using unorthodox movements to meet aggression. It is difficult at times to recognize the "true" form of your opponent because they mask their intentions, thereby confusing you. By being soft, you are flexible and more able to meet a multitude of challenges because you are yielding to others. It has also been argued that you can be forceful or unyielding at first and later agree to be yielding. Whether you are yielding at first or forceful, you must balance out your actions by maintaining an equal dose of both.

23rd Principle of Courage

The 23rd Principle of Courage teaches us that to be brave in the face of difficulty is honorable. It is easy to become fearful in situations that we cannot control. It is also natural to become fearful when we are unprepared. Courage is derived from within and it is the mind that must guide the individual to feel courageous. Courage cannot be taught, but inspiration can be shared. The reasons that stories of great and heroic deeds are shared, is so that we can draw courage instantaneously from others actions. Courage is derived from inspiration and also from a primal sense of survival. Thousands of years ago, Chinese military strategists were taught to discriminate on the battlefield and tended to focus on stratagem to deliver the victory. During the Sengoku Jedai period in Japan, Japanese military strategists spent less time discriminating and more time on advancing with their military forces in to the territories of their enemies. Within the advance, the courage is derived if not already in existence. The martial valor and courage displayed by the Samurai of the Sengoku Jedai period in Japan exemplified the model for courage on the battlefield.

24th Principle of Apprenticeship

The 24th Principle of Apprenticeship teaches us

that the best way to learn is by becoming a student of

a teacher that can guide you towards mastery in the

subject you are wishing to learn. Knowledge with its

application, is taught by a teacher who passes

knowledge on to the student, thereby conditioning the

student in the thought processes of the teacher. The

teacher is motivating the student to think like them

and learn the terminology. Information is very useful

when an application or outlet for implementation

exists. An apprentice seeks to mimic certain

behaviors, most importantly knowledge, from the mentor. The mentor as teacher is also a symbol of what the student can attain if they continue on the path of learning. It is therefore the apprentice that learns from the teacher by using similar words and phrases to sound like the teacher. The apprentice depends on the mentor's ability to not only provide personal attention, but to also discuss their insufficiencies. Although many martial arts were and still are self-taught, it was the initial phase of learning that guided them to continue training to become masters. Although the possibility exists that we may have memories linked to a greater consciousness, humans are born with a mind that is blank. We are taught by our parents or guardians, but as we grow, the need for specialists in knowledge conveyance becomes readily apparent.

In martial arts, the specialists are masters, and the students are taught according to their level of progress. Students are susceptible to ideas of suggestion and vulnerable therefore, teachers should make all efforts to be a model that is worthy of emulation. Lessons taught within the training hall, should be applied outside the training hall as well.

25th Principle of Knowledge

The 25th Principle of Knowledge teaches us

that knowledge is not bad or good, but an item to be

discovered and maintained. Knowledge is acquired

from our senses as we discover it, decode it,

categorize it, and store it. We can draw up on it at will

or it can be triggered by an emotion or a sense. It has

been recorded and stored for your retrieval, but it is

the methods for retrieval which should interest you

most. Our senses are continually devouring large

amounts of information simultaneously, but retrieval of

this is what makes it useful to us. Knowledge is also

a source of power because information is sought by

people who seek to advance. The seekers of

knowledge will always depend on those who already

invested the time to amass the knowledge. This is

because seekers of knowledge have to invest large amounts of time to learn what the learned one already has. In addition, the student may make conclusions

that are not valid and begin to believe in the "truth" of his/her own views. This is precisely why a teacher with the proper qualifications is so vital for the correct progression of a student. The teacher/mentor holds a very important place in Eastern teachings because, it it is only the teacher, that has legitimacy to distribute knowledge. Knowledge should be shared with a student based on their level of understanding, but should not be hoarded. Knowledge should be shared because the greater access individuals have to information, they better they will be equipped to make decisions. Knowledge is gained mostly from reading, listening, feeling, tasting and it is also gained from watching or observing. As an instinctual survival trait, children mimic their parents, do they not? Your own progress and possibly survival depends on your access to information does it not?

GLOSSARY

The glossary is comprised of terms from various martial arts including Chinese, Japanese, Korean, Indonesian, Greek, Filipino, and Brazilian.

KEY

American – Am

Brazilian – Br

Chinese – Ch

Filipino – Fp

French – Fr

Japanese – Jp

Korean – Kr

Russian – Ru

Thailand – Th

A

Aiki – Harmonizing with the energy of your opponent in order to control it.(Jp)

B

Ba Gua – Chinese eight trigram symbol used by Taoism and practitioners of Feng Shui. (Ch)

Bando – Burmese armed and unarmed combat system utilizing karate and judo style techniques.

Black Belt – Signifies a martial artist's expertise in a particular style; karate, judo, jujitsu, etc.

Bokken – Wooden sword. (Jp)

Brazilian Jiu-Jitsu – Brazilian martial art influenced by Pre-World War II Judo, that emphasizes ground grappling. (Br)

Bushi – Warrior. (Jp)

Bushido – Way of the Warrior (Jp)

C

Capoeira – Brazilian martial art that utilizes dance-like movements and focuses mainly on kicking techniques. (Br)

Cha Chuan – Chinese kung fu style developed by Muslims in the 14th century. (Ch)

Chagi – Kicking techniques. (Kr)

Chi – Internal Energy. Also known as Ki in Korean and Japanese. (Ch)

Chi Kung – Chinese breathing exercises used to stimulate blood circulation and to increase health.(Ch)

Chin-na – Chinese martial art that emphasizes trapping and locking techniques. (Ch)

D

Dan – Ranking. (Jp)

Dim mak – Vital point striking system that is believed to give the practicioner to be able to kill using one strike. (Ch)

Do – Way. (Jp)

Dojo – Training Hall. Literally "place of the way" (Jp)

Dumog – Filipino martial art that specializes in wrestling. (Fp)

E

Eskrima – Filipino Martial Art that uses one or two eighteen inch long bamboo sticks.(Fp)

F

Fudoshin – Calm Mind.(Jp)

G

Gi – Uniform. (Jp)

Gichin Funakoshi – Founder of Shotokan Karate. (Jp)

H

Hapkido – Korean Martial Art that blends hard strikes with submission techniques.(Kr)

Hyung – Form. (Kr)

I

Ippon – Point scored in martial arts competition. (Jp)

J

Jeet Kun Do – Martial art created by Bruce Lee. Literally means "Way of the Intercepting Fist".

Jiyu Kumite – Free Sparring. (Jp)

Jojutsu – Japanese martial art system that uses a 4 foot (1.2m) long wooden staff.(Jp)

Ju – Pliable. Flexible. Yielding. (Jp)

Judo – Japanese martial art and Olympic sport founded by Jigoro Kano in Japan.(Jp)

Jujitsu – Japanese martial art that utilizes strikes, throws, locks, submission techniques, and ground grappling. (Jp)

K

Karate – Martial Art made popular by Master Funakoshi in early 1900's Japan. (Jp)

Kata – Form or set of pre-defined movements that train the practitioners muscle memory. (Jp)

Kendo – Japanese sword fighting sport martial art in which two practitioners donning armor, use bamboo swords to defend and attack.(Jp)

Kohai – Junior leader in a martial arts school or organization. (Jp)

Krav Maga – Israeli martial art that uses effective techniques from multiple styles including judo, aikido, boxing, karate, and others.

Kumiuchi – Ancient grappling art form. (Jp)

Kung Fu – Chinese martial art that encompasses hundreds of styles. Literally means "hard work". (Ch)

Kyokushin – Karate style that emphasizes low powerful kicks. Founded by Mas Oyama. (Jp)

Kyudo – Japanese martial art that utilizes the bow and arrow with a focus on character development.(Jp)

L

Lao Tzu – Author of Tao Te Ching. (Ch)

Lua – Hawaiian martial art that specializes in bone breaking techniques.(Am)

M

Makiwara – Wooden striking post used in Karate. (Jp)

Matte – Stop. (Jp)

Muk Yan Jong – Wing Chun wooden dummy. (Ch)

Mokuso – Meditation. (Jp)

Morehei Ueshiba – Student of Sokaku Takeda. Founded Aikido or Way of Peace. (Jp)

Miyamoto Musashi – Self-taught master swordsman that dueled 60 times victoriously. (Jp)

Muay Thai – Thai Kickboxing. (Th)

N

Nage – Throwing. (Jp)

Ng Mui – Founder of the style that evolved into Wing Chun. (Ch)

Ninja –Japanese mercenary assassins that were expertly trained in stealth techniques including the murdering their opponents in their sleep.

Ninjitsu – Japanese martial art that emphasizes silent attacks, invisibility, and evasions. (Jp)

O

Osu – Greetings and respect. (Jp)

P

Pahlavani –Iranian martial art based on ancient wrestling and grappling.

Pankration – Ancient Greek martial art that used wrestling, throws, and striking techniques. (Gr)

R

Randori – Free Sparring. (Jp)

Rei – Bow. (Jp)

Ronin – A samurai that has been dismissed from service by his master. (Jp)

Ryu – Academy School. (Jp)

S

Sambo – Russian martial art influenced by judo, boxing, karate, and wrestling.(Ru)

Samurai – Feudal class of warriors during 15th century Japan. Trained in armed and unarmed combat. (Jp)

Savate – French kickboxing. (Fr)

Sempai – Senior leader in a martial arts school or organization. (Jp)

Sensei – Instructor. (Jp)

Seppuku – Ritual of self-disembowelment carried out by samurai. (Jp)

Shuai Chiao – Chinese wrestling. (Ch)

Sifu – Kung Fu Master. (Ch)

Simu – Female Kung Fu teacher. (Ch)

Sumo – Japanese Wrestling martial art. (Jp)

Systema – Russian Military Special Forces martial art created for effectiveness. (Ru)

T

Tai Chi – Martial arts system used for meditation and health by increasing blood circulation. (Ch)

Tan Tien – Stomach. Lower abdomen. (Ch)

Tao – Way. (Ch)

Tatami – Training Mat. (Jp)

Taekwondo - Korean martial art and Olympic sport that emphasizes high kicks and jumping kicks.

V

Vo Binh Dinh – Vietnamese Martial Art used for

repelling foreign invaders.

W

Waza – Technique. (Jp)

Wing Chun – Literally beautiful springtime. Effective martial art started Ng Mui, a female Shaolin master. The style uses machine-gun like rapid punches, trapping, throws, and kicks below the waist.(Ch)

Wushu – Umbrella name for Chinese martial arts. (Ch)

THE LAST WORD

Martial arts changed my life for the better by

making me healthier and happier. The changes that

materialize in a person in martial arts training stem

from the body's conditioning, effecting the individual's mental conditioning. Martial arts are comprised of many differing systems around the world, but all share the same belief in the protection of the self. By learning and training in the martial arts, you will experience many benefits that are related to such including peace of mind, mental acuity, better reflexes, less pain, a more content attitude, and better concentration. It is argued that you will live longer and have better health because of the stretching and breathing you undergo. I personally feel the positive effects of martial arts training (as does my body) and its positive health effects have been well documented. Study hard, train hard, and you will feel the change for the better.

Sincerely,

Kambiz Mostofizadeh
Author - 25 Principles of Martial Arts
www.MikazukiPublishingHouse.com

MIKAZUKI PUBLISHING HOUSE TITLES
Mikazuki Jujitsu Manual

ISBN-10: 0615473113 (Print)

ISBN-13: 9780615473116 (Print)

ISBN-10: 0615480543 (E-Book)

Author: Kambiz Mostofizadeh

Genre: Sports/Non-Fiction

Pages: 125 (Print)

Release Date: May 2011

Print Retail Price: $24.99

E-book Retail Price: $14.99

Description: Jujitsu was the battlefield art of the Samurai who used the techniques to defend themselves when they had lost their weapon and were facing an armed opponent. But in today's environment where random violence is a certainty, the knowledge of jujitsu has empowered countless individuals with the art of the samurai for self defense.

The book by Kambiz Mostofizadeh is a jujitsu manual explaining core jujitsu techniques, shares the principles and applications of ju or yielding, covers Jujitsu's Japanese origins, teaches methods for fighting against multiple attackers, includes techniques for defeating mixed martial artists, and divulges strategies for offensive and defensive maneuvers. The book features more than 20 hand drawn illustrations representing the various techniques used within jujitsu. Mikazuki Jujitsu Manual; Learn Jujitsu also features a glossary of jujitsu terms, annual jujitsu tournaments, and methods for defeating a boxer. The author said "I wrote this book as a guide for my students and any student of modern martial arts. I believe all people can benefit from the study of martial arts, because the need for personal safety and protection is essential to everyone".

Karate 360

ISBN-10: 0983594627 (Print)

ISBN-13: 9780983594628 (Print)

ISBN-13: 978-0-9835946-7-3 (E-book)

Author: Kambiz Mostofizadeh

Genre: Sports/Non-Fiction

Print Retail Price: $14.99

E-book Retail Price: $4.99

Pages: 115 (Print)

Release Date: December 2011

Description: Explore Karate's roots, learn key karate techniques, and learn why Karate is the world's most popular martial art.

EXCERPT - "The essence of Karate is defense. The powerful leg strikes, efficient blocking techniques, and strong punches evolved in to an effective martial art that eventually became the most popular martial art in the world".

25 Principles of Martial Arts

ISBN-13: 9780983594604 (Print)

ISBN-10: 0983594619 (E-Book)

Author: Kambiz Mostofizadeh

Genre: Philosophy/Non-Fiction

Pages: 111 (Print)

Release Date: November 2011

Print Retail Price: $14.99

E-book Retail Price: $7.99

EXCERPT - "Large amount of resources and more individuals in your organization do not necessarily equate to victory over your opponent if you have lost the advantage of formlessness."

Description: Learn the 25 key principles of martial arts and the strategies that make them successful. This book divulges strategies and tactics that can be applied in the dojo, in your personal life, and in your business affairs.

Letting the Customers Win

ISBN-10: 0983594651 (Print)

ISBN-13: 9780983594659 (Print)

ISBN-13: 978-0-9835946-8-0 (E-book)

Author: Kambiz Mostofizadeh

Genre: Business/Non-Fiction

Pages: 120

Release Date: February 2011

Print Retail Price: $14.99

E-book Retail Price: $9.99

Description: Millions of dollars are spent to attract customers, while little is spent to keep current customers happy. It is 7 more times expensive to gain new business than it is to keep your current customer. This book reveals customer care strategies including call center management, customer loyalty card schemes, and relationship marketing.

Find the Ideal Husband

ISBN-10: 0983594694 (E-book)

ISBN-13: 9780983594697 (E-book)

Author: Kambiz Mostofizadeh

Genre: Self-help/Non-Fiction

Pages: 110 (E-book)

Release Date: Valentine's Day 2012

E-book Retail Price: $9.99

Description: The ideal husband is rich, classy, happy, handsome, and caring. Learn where to meet the ideal husband and how to recognize the indicators for knowing he is the right choice. Let the search begin!

Learning Magic

ISBN-10: 0983594635 (Print)

ISBN-13: 978-0983594635 (Print)

Author: Kambiz Mostofizadeh

Genre: Performing Arts/Non-Fiction

Pages: 111 (Print)

Release Date: March 2012

Print Retail Price: $14.99

Description: Learn the fundamentals of performing magic including the reasons why magic tricks are so effective. Whether at home, in the office, or at a gathering, this book will teach you key magic tricks for performing.

Political Advertising Manual

ISBN-10: 0983594643 (Print)

ISBN-13: 9780983594642 (Print)

ISBN-13: 978-0-9835946-8-0 (E-book)

Author: Kambiz Mostofizadeh

Genre: Political Science/Non-Fiction

Pages: 119 (Print)

Release Date: Jan 2012

Print Retail Price: $14.99

E-book Retail Price: $9.99

Description: Political marketing strategies are used by nearly every victorious candidate to achieve electoral victory. Explore key political marketing techniques & tactics for effective message delivery.

Street Food War

ISBN-13: 9781937981006 (Print)

ISBN-13: 978-1-937981-98-3 (E-book)

Author: Kambiz Mostofizadeh

Genre: Food & Culinary Arts/Non-Fiction

Pages: 125 (Print)

Release Date: February 2012

Print Retail Price: $12.99

E-book Retail Price: $7.99

Description: There are millions of food trucks, food carts, and food stalls in the U.S. The fantastic growth of street food and its popularity in television shows, has drawn the interest of millions to the benefits of quality street food. Go behind the scenes of the street food industry and learn how it operates. This is the must-have guide for anyone that loves street food or works in the street food industry.

Living the Pirate Code

ISBN-13: 9781937981013 (Print)

ISBN-13: 9781937981020 (E-book)

Author: Eric Hurtado

Genre: History/Non-Fiction

Pages: 200 (Print)

Release Date: March 2012

Print Retail Price: $19.99

E-book Retail Price: $9.99

Description: Pirates were famous sailors who hunted for gold and treasure. Learn the famous code practiced by pirates and how this impacted their lives. Discover the greatest pirates and how they shaped our modern history.

More Titles Coming Soon

Visit www.MikazukiPublishingHouse.com for more information on our books.

Mikazuki Publishing House is a book publishing

company specializing in a variety of non-fiction works.

Press Contacts interested in arranging press interviews and/or author appearances, are welcome to contact:

pr@MikazukiPublishingHouse.com for info

三日月

We believe that the written word is the most effective vehicle for the delivery of knowledge and that reading is essential to educating oneself. Mikazuki Publishing House believes in the promotion of reading as a tool for self progression and therefore invests resources, working with libraries and institutions of higher learning, to propagate the advantages of reading. Mikazuki Publishing House also offers free book donations and free book signings/appearances to libraries upon request (upon availability).

Mikazuki Publishing House is honored to be an active participant in the fight to reverse world deforestation. Approximately 30 million trees are cut down in the U.S. every year to be used for the creation of print books.

We wish to offset and counterbalance the use of paper in the book publishing industry by working with organizations dedicated to reversing the trend of world deforestation.

We will first start with one tree. The consequences of not doing so could be disastrous for future generations.

Every minute over 160 acres of land feel the destructive effects of deforestation. Deforestation causes species to become extinct, disrupts natural habitats, and erodes the top soil of viable farming lands causing drought and famine.

As a responsible book publisher, Mikazuki Publishing House will donate a percentage from the sale of each book to the effort of planting millions of trees.

Mikazuki Publishing House is pleased to invite foundations, associations, and groups dedicated to planting trees to contact us.

Please send all requests to:

philanthropy@MikazukiPublishingHouse.com

Mikazuki Publishing House enables greater exchange of knowledge by providing our authors to public institutions as guest speakers.

As well as guest speaking, our authors will give personal time to each fan when also conducting a book signing.

As our authors have limited time due to writing and book tours, we ask that you submit a request outlining the type of event with its pertinent information included.

We invite requests from the following types of organizations:

Public Libraries/Book Fairs

Event Management organizations

Community Centers

Community Colleges/Universities

Book Clubs with over 50 Active members

Please send all requests to:
philanthropy@MikazukiPublishingHouse.com

Mikazuki Publishing House is a proud member of the Independent Book Publishers Association

NOTES ON 25 PRINCIPLES
OF MARTIAL ARTS
(Please use for taking notes or commenting on this book)

NOTES ON 25 PRINCIPLES
OF MARTIAL ARTS
(Please use for taking notes or commenting on this book)

NOTES ON 25 PRINCIPLES OF MARTIAL ARTS

(Please use for taking notes or commenting on this book)

NOTES ON 25 PRINCIPLES OF MARTIAL ARTS

(Please use for taking notes or commenting on this book)

NOTES ON 25 PRINCIPLES
OF MARTIAL ARTS
(Please use for taking notes or commenting on this book)

NOTES ON 25 PRINCIPLES OF MARTIAL ARTS

(Please use for taking notes or commenting on this book)

NOTES ON 25 PRINCIPLES
OF MARTIAL ARTS

(Please use for taking notes or commenting on this book)